# MY FAVORITE FILIPINO FOODS FROM A to Z

Written and Illustrated by Anne Castro

I dedicate this book to all of the amazing women in my family. Thank you for always inspiring me to be my authentic self.

## Adobo

**Adobo** can be made with chicken or pork.
Eat it with rice and your spoon and fork.
Soy sauce, vinegar, garlic, and bay leaf to season.
There are peppercorns too. You don't eat those for good reason.

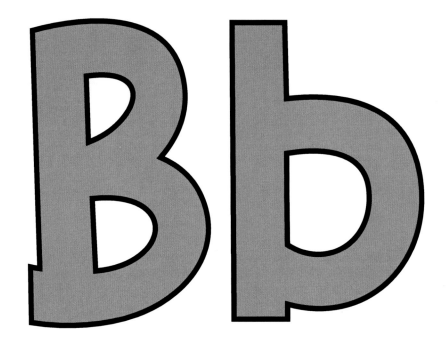

## Biko

**Biko**, **bibingka**, and **buko** all start with B.
They're much too delicious to not mention all three.
**Buko** means young coconut, and with sweet rice it's yummy.
Eating these desserts makes me rub my tummy.

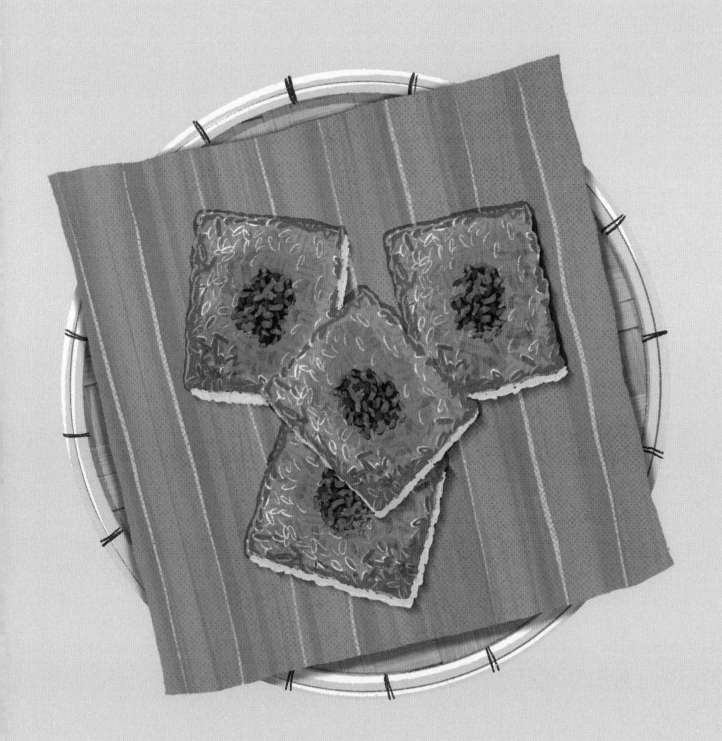

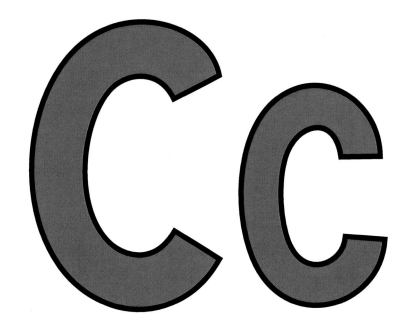

# Champorado

**Champorado** has chocolate,
adding milk makes it creamy.
And of course it has rice!
Serve it cold, or hot and steamy.

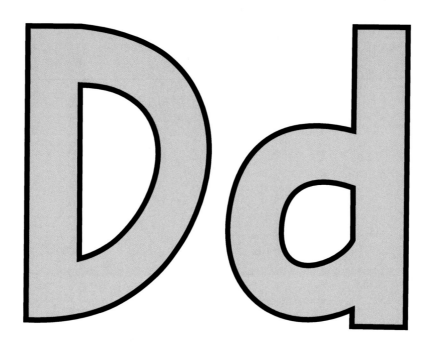

## DURIAN

**Durian** is a fruit that has spikes and a stink,
but it tastes a lot better than you'd probably think.
Cut open to see the yummy fruit treat.
You might be surprised that it's actually sweet.

# ENSAYMADA

**Ensaymada** is a pastry that you surely must try.
It's fluffy. It's moist. It's delicious, that's why!
It's bread covered in cheese. It's buttery too.
It's sugary and simply too good to be true!

# FLAN

F is for Leche **Flan**, another sweet treat.
Once you see the glisten, it's hard not to eat.
The top is so rich, caramel-y, and gold.
It's the type of dessert that never gets old.

# Gg

## Ginataan

**Ginataan** means "made with coconut milk",
A general term all Pinoys know.
My favorite is **Ginataang Bilo Bilo***,
made with Tapioca, rice balls, plantain, and sweet potato.

bilO* ball

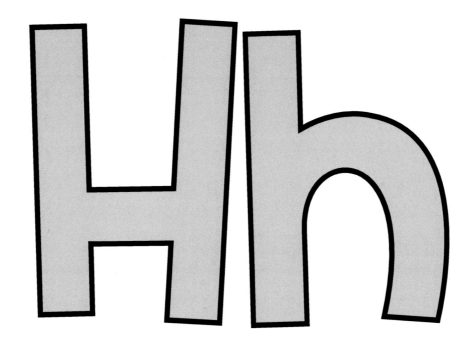

## Halo-Halo

**Halo-halo** in English, translates to "Mix-mix".
It's every Filipino's go-to dessert fix.
You can use ice cream or milk with shaved ice,
add jello, beans, fruit... even crispy flat rice

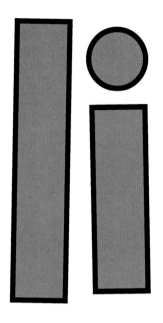

# INihaw

I is for **Inihaw**, Filipino BBQ.
It's a plate full to feed an entire crew.
Sausages, skewers, and sizzling meats.
It's more than a meal, it's a full-blown feast!

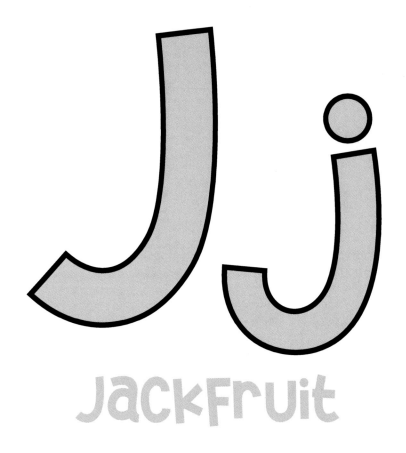

## Jackfruit

**Jackfruit** is similar to durian,
but not quite as scary.
It's less spiky and doesn't smell,
despite the contrary.

## kare-kare

**Kare-Kare** is a thick peanut stew,
with tender meat and veggies too.
Like string beans, bokchoy, and eggplant slices,
and shrimp paste and all of our typical spices.

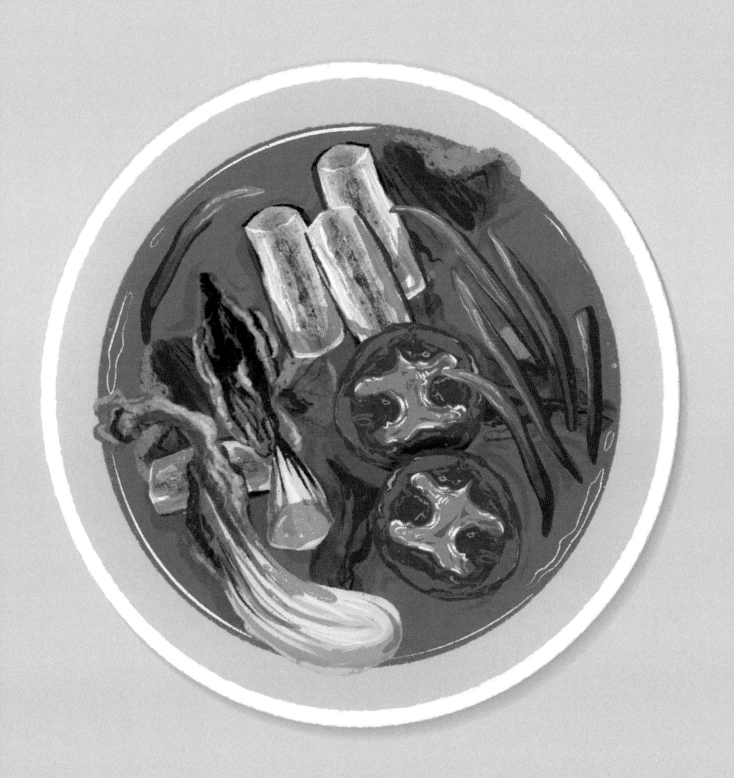

# Lugaw & Lumpia

**Lugaw** is a porridge with chicken and rice.
Add garlic, ginger, egg, and green onion to taste nice.
**Lumpia** is a fried spring roll that also has meat.
A crowd favorite that everyone will surely eat.

## Manga

**Manga**, or **mango**, is a favorite island fruit.
Not only is it good, but it's good for you too!
Dip it in **bagoong\*** and give it a taste.
It gives a burst of flavor that you surely won't waste.

**bagoong\*** a condiment made of fermented fish, krill, or shrimp paste with salt

## Nilaga

**Nilaga** is a soupy stew for a cold, rainy day.
The type of dish to make all your worries go away.
We Filipinos love soup that make us feel warm,
A delicious, feel-good stew to help weather any storm.

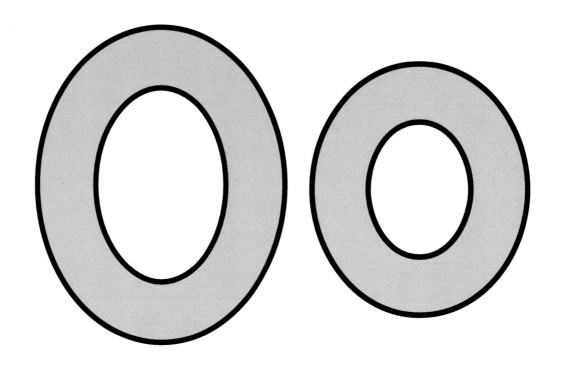

## Okoy

**Okoy**, or **ukoy**, are fried fritters made crisp.
A shrimp and veggie batter you mix with a whisk.
Often times dipped in **suka**\* to make it a bit sour.
Okoy is delicious any time of the hour!

suka\* Filipino vinegar

# Palabok

**Palabok** is a noodle dish that my Lola always makes,
with boiled egg, shrimp, chicharon, and tinapa flakes.
We always have noodles on special days for good fortune.
A long life to live, so go get a good portion!

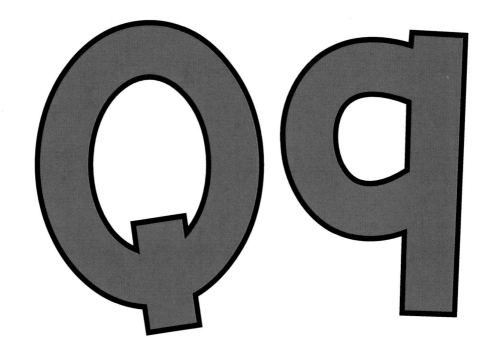

# Queso Ice Cream

**Queso\* Ice Cream** is yummy, I promise.
It won't make you feel queasy.
The perfect mix of salty and sweet,
even if it sounds cheesy!

QUESO\* Filipino/Spanish for cheese

## Rice

R is for **Rice**, **on kanin**, we could never forget.
Without this staple, our table isn't set.
We love it plain or drenched in **sabaw***.
To live without it, we wouldn't know how!

sabaw* soup, sauce, or gravy poured on rice

# Sisig

**Sisig** is a delicacy that tastes both savory and sweet,
and spicy if you like to add peppers for heat.
It's crispy chopped pork that's best with a sizzle,
and even a bit tangy with **calamansi\*** drizzle!

**calamansi\*** small citrus fruit similar to a lime

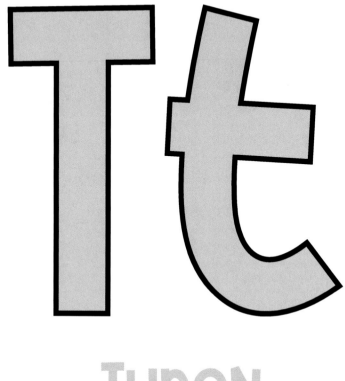

Turon

**Turon** is wrapped banana fried in a brown sugar roll.
A sweet crispy dessert that's good for the soul.
If you bring it to a potluck, it's sure to be a winner,
the talk of the party after everyone's dinner!

## Ube

**Ube** is one of our favorite flavors.
A purple yam that is made into so many favors.
Ice cream, jam, pastries, and more,
the flavor, the color, what else could you ask for?

# Vinegar

**Vinegar**, or **suka**, makes our food taste great,
a famous ingredient for any Pinoy plate.
Onions, garlic, and peppers perk up the flavor.
Once you try our special suka, it's the ultimate savor!

# WANSOY

**Wansoy** is **cilantro** used to decorate a dish.
Brighten up any taste as much as you wish.
Sometimes the leaf can be put on the top,
or to mix it in, it can also be chopped.

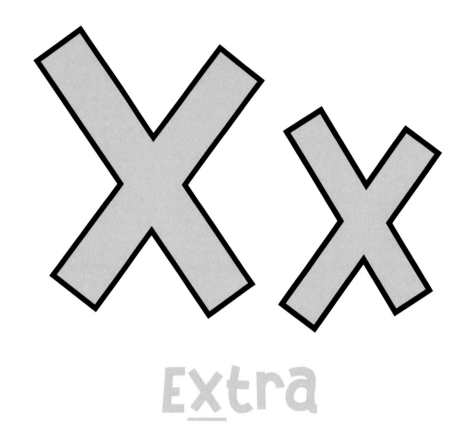

## E<u>x</u>tra

X is for **Ex<u>t</u>ra**, a word Pinoys love.
You can always have more if push comes to shove.
Extra rice, extra soup, we always make plenty.
If you visit our house, your tummy will never be empty.

## yema

Don't forget to save room for a few **yema** goodies,
a delicious dessert for all of you foodies.
It's a candy made with egg yolk, sugar, and milk.
It's sweet, yet simple, and smooth like silk!

I could really catch some **Z**s after all of these foods.
They say after you eat, you have the best snooze!
I'll be dreaming of buko and ube delights,
so sweet dreams for now, 'til we have our next bite!

Can you spot the differences between
the English Alphabet and the Filipino Alphabet?
Some letters are missing, some letters are new.
Read them aloud and you might learn a few.

# The Filipino Alphabet

A (Ah)

B (Ba)

K (Ka)

D (Da)

E (Eh)

G (Ga)

H (Ha)

I (Ih)

L (La)

M (Ma)

N (Na)

NG (Nga)

O (Oh)

P (Pa)

R (Ra)

S (Sa)

T (Ta)

U (ōō)

W (Wa)

Y (Ya)

Made in the USA
Las Vegas, NV
27 December 2024

15405607R00036